What's on the Washing Line?

Written and illustrated by
Andrew Midgley

Collins Educational
An imprint of HarperCollinsPublishers

Aunty Anila's Assorted Aprons

Bobby's Bright Blue Beret

Cathy's Confiscated Catapult Collection

Daphne's Dismal Dressmaking Disaster

Eskimo Eric's Enormous Earmuffs

Fashionable Freddie's Fluorescent Footwear

Gilbert's Grubby Green Gardening Gloves

Henry's Horrible Holey Handkerchief

Isaac's Itchy Imitation Identity

Jokey Jack's Jazzy Jacket

Katie's Knitted Keep-fit Koala

Lucy's Lengthy Lilac Leggings

Mei Mei's Microscopic Magenta Mittens

Nancy's New Nylon Nightie

Ozzy's Only Orange Octopus

Pippa's Pink Polkadot Pullover

Queenie's Quotable Quilt

Ruby's Rubbery Red Raincoat

Susie's Stripy Swimsuit

Timothy's Terrible Technicolour Tie

Uncle Ulysses' Unshrinkable Underwear

Victor's Voluminous Violet Vest

Wally's Woolly Winter Waistcoat

Xavier's Xmassy X-ray Specs

Yvonne's Yellow Yo-yo

Zoe's Zany Zigzaggy Zebra